The Tony Blair
New Labour
Joke Book

The word 'politics' is derived from the words 'poly' meaning many, and the word 'tics' meaning blood-sucking parasites. Funnily enough, we also have a New Labour Government.

Also by Iain Dale and published by Robson Books

As I Said to Denis: The Margaret Thatcher Book of Questions
The Blair Necessities: The Tony Blair Book of Quotations
The Unofficial Book of Political Lists
The Bill Clinton Joke Book – Uncensored
The Wit and Wisdom of Tony Banks

The Tony Blair New Labour Joke Book

Compiled by
Iain Dale & John Simmons
Cartoons by David Haselhurst

 Robson Books

For Jan, Jason, Stephanie and Daniel

First published in Great Britain in 1999 by Robson Books, 10 Blenheim Court, Brewery Road, London N7 9NT

A member of the Chrysalis Group plc

British Library Cataloguing in Publication Data
A catalogue record for this title is available from the British Library

ISBN 1 86105 271 5

Printed and bound in Great Britain by Creative Print and Design (Wales), Ebbw Vale

Acknowledgements

New Labour has become a political phenomenon. Tony Blair has had the longest political honeymoon in living memory and in this book we salute him and his colleagues for their contribution to political satire. All governments, whatever their political colours, fall victim to the satirists and comedians. In a democracy it is only right and proper that they should do so. Just as Margaret Thatcher and John Major were ridiculed and lampooned, now it is the turn of Blair, Prescott, Cook and Brown.

We would like to record our thanks to all those who have contributed material for this book – in particular Julian White, who maintains the British Politics Homepage on the Internet (www.ukpol.co.uk). Thanks also to William Tunstall-Pedoe and his anagram website. We would also like to mention our colleagues at Politico's Bookstore whom we have probably driven mad during the compilation of this slight but perfectly formed tome. Our thanks go to John Berry, Sarah Harvey, Danny Clark, Simon Marcus and Renah Valeh. We are also grateful to Matthew Parris for giving permission to reprint two of his excellent articles. Thanks also go to William Bike, and to David Haselhurst for his excellent illustrations.

Iain Dale and John Simmons
July 1999

Top Ten Campaign Promises Tony Blair Is Sorry He Made

1 To bomb France back to the First Republic
2 To privatize the British Library through QVC
3 To bring more lightweight pretty boys into the Party
4 To reveal at first Prime Minister's Questions John Prescott's IQ
5 To abandon the use of verbs
6 To invite Tony Booth to the victory celebrations
7 To give an interview to Dr Ruth
8 Not to raise taxes
9 A referendum on PR – The Lib Dems can go to hell
10 To make Frank Dobson Secretary of State for Health

A long time ago, Leo Blair and his wife had a son, who was still living with his parents. The parents were a little worried, as the son was still unable to decide about his career path so they decided to do a small test.

They took a ten-pound note, a Bible, and a bottle of whisky, and put them on the front hall table. Then they hid, hoping he would think they weren't at home.

The father told the mother, 'If he takes the money he will be a businessman, if he takes the Bible he will be a priest – but if he takes the bottle of whisky, I'm afraid our son will be a drunkard.'

So the parents took their place in the nearby closet and waited nervously. Peeping through the keyhole they saw their son arrive home. He saw the note they had left, saying they'd be home later. Then, he took the ten-pound note, looked at it against the light, and slid it in his pocket.

After that, he took the Bible, flicked through it, and took it also.

Finally, he grabbed the bottle, opened it, and took an appreciative whiff to be assured of the quality. Then he left for his room, carrying all the three items.

The father slapped his forehead, and said: 'WOW! It's even worse than I ever imagined ...'

'What do you mean?' his wife inquired.

'Tony is going to be a politician!' replied the concerned father.

Tony Blair and Gordon Brown were taking a wander through St James Park.

'Look,' said Tony to Gordon, 'Let's be honest with each other.'

'Okay, you first,' said Gordon.

That was the end of the discussion.

Tony Blair and Gordon Brown were walking through the woods when they spotted a vicious-looking bear. Tony immediately opened his briefcase, pulled out a pair of trainers and started putting them on.

Gordon looked at him and said, 'You're crazy! You'll never be able to outrun that bear!'

'I don't have to,' said Tony. 'I only have to outrun you.'

Robin Cook's mother gets on a bus holding the cherub Robin in her arms. The bus driver says, 'That's the ugliest baby I've ever seen.' In a huff, Mrs Cook slammed her fare into the fare box and took an aisle seat near the rear of the bus. The man seated next to her sensed that she was agitated and asked her what was wrong. 'The bus driver insulted me,' she fumed.

The man sympathized and said: 'That's terrible – he's a public servant and shouldn't say things to insult passengers.'

'You're right,' she said. 'I think I'll go back up there and give him a piece of my mind.'

'That's a good idea,' the man said. 'Here, let me hold your monkey.'

The morning after a big party in honour of the French Culture Minister, Tony Banks was nursing a king-size hangover and finding his memory a bit hazy, asked his wife: 'What the hell happened last night?'

She shuddered. 'As usual you made a complete tosser of yourself in front of Chris Smith,' replied the long suffering Mrs Banks.

'Oh, piss on him them,' answered Banks.

'You did,' said his wife.

'He fired you.'

Banks grunted. 'Well, fuck him then.'

'You did,' she replied, 'and he gave you your job back.'

The Cabinet were in a plane. Tony Blair decides to throw one five-pound note out to make someone happy. Not to be outdone, Gordon Brown throws two five pounds out to make two people happy (remembering to claim the money back from the Treasury). The pilot looks back and says, 'Why don't you chuck yourselves out and make 58 million people happy?'.

Last winter Tony Blair was going for his jog when he noticed 'Die Blair, Die' written in urine in the snow.

He had the police analyse the writing. They said that they had good news and they had bad news.

Smiling Tony said, 'Well, give me the good news first.'

They said the good news is that it was William Hague's urine.

'What!', he exclaimed, if that is the good news, then what could be the bad?

They replied, 'It was Gordon Brown's handwriting.'

Quasimodo asks Esmerelda one day if he really is the ugliest man alive. Esmerelda says, 'Go upstairs and ask the magic mirror who is the ugliest man alive and the magic mirror will tell you.'

Five minutes later, Quasimodo comes back and sits down. After a while, Esmerelda says, 'Well?'

To which Quasimodo says, 'Who's Robin Cook?'

Top Ten Good Things About Being Deputy Prime Minister

1 All the fun with none of the responsibility
2 Allowed to pick any voter at random and spend their taxes on whatever you like
3 You're not married to Cherie
4 Get to pretend to be PM when Tony's away
5 Er, that's it

Robin Cook and his then wife Margaret had been married for 20 years. When they first got married Robin said, 'I am putting a box under the bed. You must promise never to look in it.' In all their 40 years of marriage Margaret never looked. However on the afternoon of their 20th anniversary curiosity got the best of her and she lifted the lid and peeked inside. In the box were three empty beer cans and £1,874.25 in cash. She closed the box and put it back under the bed.

Now that she knew what was in the box, she was doubly curious as to why. That evening they were out for a special dinner. After dinner Margaret could no longer contain her curiosity and she confessed, saying, 'I am so sorry Robin. For all these years I kept my promise and never looked into the box under our bed. However, today the temptation was too much and I gave in. But now I need to know why do you keep the cans in the box?'

Robin thought for a while and said, 'I guess after all these years you deserve to know the truth. Whenever I was unfaithful to you I put an empty beer can in the box under the bed to remind myself not to do it again.'

Margaret was shocked, but said, 'I am very disappointed and saddened but I guess after all those years away from home on the road, temptation does happen and I guess that three times is not that bad considering the years.'

They hugged and made their peace. A little while later

Margaret asked Robin, 'Why do you have all that money in the box?'

Robin answered, 'Whenever the box filled with empties, I cashed them in.'

Top Ten Signs You're in Love With a Politician

1 When you see him on TV and you start licking the screen
2 You call the Parliamentary Channel requesting a tape of his greatest speeches
3 Your dog's name is Big Ben
4 You write to the Queen suggesting his birthday is declared a national holiday
5 You just luuuurve those double chins
6 You're turned on by the sight of his despatch box
7 You buy up remaindered copies of his memoirs so his feelings won't be hurt
8 You tell all your friends that his wife just doesn't understand him
9 You spend all your holidays in his constituency
10 You'd give him your last Rolo

Did you hear that Robin Cook is so ugly that people put his picture in their car window as an anti-theft device?

Q: What will Tony Blair do after he dies?
A: He'll lie still.

Q: What's the difference between Christmas and Election Day?
A: On Christmas Day you get a turkey for a day, on Election Day you get a turkey for five years.

Q: Why is New Labour like cannabis?
A: Both induce mild euphoria and a distorted sense of reality. Both induce a tendency to talk rubbish in a meaningful way. With both, everything takes on added significance despite the fact that nothing is happening.

Q: What do you have if you've got John Prescott, Harriet Harman and Dolly Parton all in the same room?

A: Two boobs and a country singer.

Q: How do you confuse John Prescott?

A: Ask him a question.

John Prescott and Frank Dobson were out hunting when they came upon a couple of tracks. After close examination, John declared them to be deer tracks. Frank disagreed, insisting they must be elk tracks.

They were still arguing when the train hit them.

John Prescott and Peter Mandelson were both driving back from Chequers when they ran into each other. Peter saw John was a little shaken up, and offered him a drink of some whisky that he happened to have with him. John said, 'Thanks Peter, that's really nice of you, why don't you have some too?'.

Mandelson turned away, took out his mobile and dialled 999 and muttered: 'Sure John, sure, but only after the police leave.'

Did you hear that Gordon Brown got a fax from John Prescott? He knew it was from John because there was a stamp on it.

Q: Did you hear John Prescott had got a pet zebra?
A: He called it spot.

Did you hear that John Prescott was in a supermarket and saw the sign, 'Wet Floor'. So he unzipped his trousers and did exactly that.

Q: How do you tell if John Prescott has been using the new Cabinet Minister's computer network?
A: There's Tippex on the monitor screen.

Q: How do you keep John Prescott busy?
A: Write 'Please turn over' on both sides of a piece of paper.

Q: How do you confuse John Prescott?
A: You don't, he's born that way.

Q: How do you keep John Prescott busy all day?
A: Put him in a round room and tell him to sit in a corner.

Q: Why did John Prescott stare at a carton of orange juice for two hours?
A: Because it said concentrate.

Einstein, Casals, Picasso and John Prescott die and go to heaven. St Peter is waiting for them, and requests identification. Einstein, who is first in line, says, 'I don't have any ID, but I can explain the equivalence of matter and energy.' He is given a blackboard and proceeds to give an eloquent explanation of one of his most famous theories. 'Only Einstein himself could explain this so well,' says St Peter. 'Step right in, professor. Next?'

Then Casals, who is next in line, says, 'I don't have any ID, but I can play my cello to prove who I am.' He is given a cello and plays the most beautiful music imaginable.

'There's no question, you must be Casals,' says St Peter. 'Next?'

Picasso steps to the gate. 'I don't have any ID, but I can paint a picture to prove who I am.' He is given some brushes and paints a spectacular picture.

'Okay, you're Picasso. Go right ahead,' says St Peter. 'Next?'

'I'm John Prescott,' says the smiling former Deputy Prime Minister, 'but I don't have any ID. How can I prove who I am?'

'Well,' says St Peter. 'Einstein was just here, and he discussed some of this theories. Then there was Casals , who played the cello for us. Then Picasso came, and he painted a picture. Can you do anything like that?'

'Who are Einstein, Casals, and Picasso?' asks Prescott. St Peter looks at him and says, 'Mr Prescott, go right in.'

One day John Prescott was visiting the Queen and she decided to take him for a tour of London in the royal carriage. Now the carriage was being pulled by six royal stallions and one of them suddenly passed wind. It sounded like a 21-gun salute it was so loud. The smell permeated the inside of the carriage and the Queen was totally devastated.

'I apologize profusely for the terrible smell inside the carriage,' she said.

'Oh, that's all right', said Prescott, 'for a minute there I thought it was the horse.'

Peter Mandelson awoke in a hospital bed after a complicated operation, and found that the curtains were drawn around him. 'Why are the curtains closed?' he said. 'Is it night?'

A nurse replied, 'No, it is just that there is a fire across the street, and we didn't want you waking up and thinking that the operation was unsuccessful.'

The Bosnian peace talks continue. The only thing that Alija Izetbegovic, Radovan Karadzic and Slobodan Milosovic could agree on was that Tony Blair has a funny name.

Q: What's the similarity between Robin Cook and a three pin plug?
A: They're both no good in Europe.

Top Ten Old Labour Political Turn Ons

1 Tony Benn
2 Mushy peas
3 Whippets
4 Flat caps
5 Miners
6 Sheffield
7 Dennis Skinner's eyes
8 Glorious election defeats
9 Alma Sedgwick
10 Marx's *Das Kapital*

A young man needed a new brain for his brain transplant. He was offered one of a university professor, the other of Harriet Harman. The former cost £10,000, but the brain of Harriet Harman cost a cool million.

The young man said, 'I didn't realize Harriet Harman's brain was so much better'.

The doctor said, 'Oh, it isn't better, just unused.'

When Margaret Beckett was born, her mother said, 'What a treasure.' Her dad took one look and said, 'Yep, let's go and bury it.'

A mid-level executive was so frustrated at being passed over for promotion year after year, that, in frustration, he went to a brain-transplant centre in the hope of raising his IQ 20 points.

After a battery of physical and psychological tests, he was told by the centre's director that he was an acceptable candidate.

'That's great!' the executive said. 'But I understand that this procedure can be really expensive.'

'Yes, sir, it can,' the director replied. 'An ounce of accountant's brain for example, costs £1,000; an ounce of an economist's brain costs £2,000; an ounce of a corporate president's is £45,000. An ounce of a New Labour's brain is £75,000.'

'£75,000 for an ounce of a New Labour's brain? Why on earth is that?'

'Do you have any idea,' the director asked, 'how many MPs we would have to kill?'

When Margaret Beckett was a baby they had to put her in an incubator with tinted windows.

Tony Blair is a real politician – willing to do anything for the working classes except join them.

If John Prescott is so keen on reducing air pollution, why doesn't he stop making speeches?

Have you seen the New Labour candidate doll? When you wind it up, its mouth opens and closes, but it doesn't say anything.

After a gruelling Prime Minister's Question Time Tony Blair was walking back to Downing Street when a man rushed up to him and exclaimed: 'Prime Minister – you were brilliant! I particularly liked the straightforward way in which you dodged the issue.'

Q: Why do these new trendies say they're from the New Left?
A: Because they're so far from being right.

Tony Blair is a typical politician. He spends half his time making promises and the other half making excuses.

Tony Blair's ABC

In his *Times* column, Matthew Parris devised an ABC Guide to Blair-speak. He wrote in July 1994: 'Labour MPs hoping for a job under the new leader would be wise to draw their speeches and their tone from this lexicon. Get ahead of the pack: get in tune with Tony now.' As ever, Matthew was ahead of his time...

A is for Achievement. Achievements are one of the main things a Blair government will achieve. A is also for Abstract. Abstract nouns are another Blair achievement. A is for Absolutely too. 'Absolutely' means 'yes' in Islington.

B is for Beliefs. Politics is about beliefs. B is for Basic. Basic beliefs. B is for Broader society. And B is for the Battle of Ideas. 'Only by re-establishing its core identity can the Labour Party regain the intellectual self-confidence to take on and win the Battle of Ideas (Fabian/*Guardian* Conference, 18 June 1994).

C is for Core Identity; also Core beliefs; also Community,

Citizenship, Cohesion, Compassion, Confidence, Coalition and Change.

D is for Duty: 'individuals owe a Duty to one another and to a broader society (*ibid*). D is also for Direction, new Direction, and Drive in a new direction.

E is for Energy: 'the power and Energy of ideas and vision' (*ibid*). E is for Equality, too. 'Social Justice. Cohesion, Equality of opportunity and community' (*ibid*) and for Ethical Socialism, as distinguished from unethical socialism.

F is for fairness, for Freedom and for Full employability.

G is for Global: 'First, the economy is Global' (*ibid*). Labour's foreign and defence policy are also likely to be Global.

H is for Historic mission. Also for Historic opportunity: 'A Historic opportunity now to give leadership' (*ibid*).

I is for Initiative. No minister will be without one. As well as Initiatives, a Blair administration will have Ideas. 'The future will be decided…through the power and energy of Ideas and vision' (*ibid*).

J is for Justice and social Justice (*see* Ethical Socialism).

K is for Key values and also for key beliefs (*see also* Core values and Core beliefs). 'Socialism as defined by certain

Key values and beliefs is not merely alive, it has a historic opportunity now to give Leadership' (*ibid*).

L is for Leadership (*see* Historic opportunity/Key values).

M is for Modern: 'a future that is both radical and Modern (*ibid*). M is for Movement, too: 'a radical Movement in this country for change and national renewal' (*ibid*).

N is for National renewal.

O is for Opportunity: '…the chance to capture the entire ground and language of Opportunity (*ibid*. *See also* Equality).

P is for Partnership. P is also for Purpose, Power, Potential and Pluralism: 'a greater Pluralism of ideas and thought' (*ibid*).

Q is for Quality work. 'Central to my belief about this country is that we've got to give people the chance not to work, but actually to have Quality work' (Interview with David Frost, 12 June 1994).

R is for Rediscovery, Responsibilities, Realisation and Respect: 'We do need to Rediscover a strong sense of civic and community values, the belief that we must combine opportunities and Responsibilities, and the Realisation that true self-respect can come only through respect for others' (Speech to the CBI, 14 June 1994).

S is for Society; and plural Society, and shared Society, and broader Society, and changed Society, and Social... and 'Social -*ism* – if you will (Fabian/*Guardian* Conference, 18 June 1994).

T is for Tough: 'Tough on crime, Tough on the causes of crime'. T is also for Thinking, Thought, Trust and True self-respect.

U is for Urgency. U is also for United: 'a strong, United society which gives each citizen the chance to develop their potential to the full (*ibid. See also* Society).

V is for Values. For Vigour and Victory too; and, more than all else, V is for Vision: ' a central Vision based around principle but liberated from particular policy prescriptions...' (*ibid*). You can say that again!

W is for Worth: 'the equal Worth of each citizen' (*ibid*). W is also for Welfare and Wellbeing.

X is for X factor. John Major doesn't have it, according to a survey conducted for Mazda cars, Tony Blair has Factor X.

Y is for Youth. Blair has that, too.

Z is for Zero-sum game. A Zero-sum game is a calculation in which if you add to one thing you must take it away from another. Blair's economics, as he has said, is *not* a Zero-sum game. This means that you can have your cake and eat it.

Interviewer: So what's your position on Red China?

New Labour MP: I'm all in favour of it…as long as it doesn't clash with the rest of the decor

The dangerous thing about New Labour jokes is that some of them get elected.

Gordon Brown knows exactly what he's doing. He puts up the tax on beer and spirits, which drives us all to drink!

Did you hear they're adding two more faces to Mount Rushmore?
Tony Blair's.

Three kids are walking by a lake. They see Tony Blair out jogging, and he falls into the lake. They go and save him from drowning. Then he says that he will give them anything they want.

He asks the first boy what he wants, and he says, 'I want to go to Oxford University.'

Blair says, 'Don't worry, I'll fix it for you.'

He asks the second child, and he says he wants to go to Cambridge.

Blair says he will have a word with David Blunkett.

He asks what the third boy wants. He says, 'I want to be buried in Westminster Abbey.'

Blair says: 'You are so young, why are you concerned about when you are going to die.

The boy says, 'Because my father will kill me when he finds out what I did!'

Meteorologists say that it is now possible to predict the winner of the next General Election by the weather. According to the historical records, if the election is held on a cold, wet day, then Tony Blair will have the best chance of winning. If the weather is warm and sunny, then William Hague has the edge. And, of course, if it's a cold day in hell, the Liberal Democrats will win.

Q: What's the difference between movie producer Oliver Stone and Tony Blair?

A: Stone gets rich lying about the past, Blair gets elected lying about the future.

Q: How are a beer bottle and Frank Dobson the same?

A: They are both empty from the neck up.

As Tony Blair was walking on a beach one day, his foot tripped on a partially buried bottle. Picking it up, he rubbed it to expose the label. Suddenly a cloud poured from the bottle and a huge genie appeared.

'Thank you – oh, thank you for saving me from the prison I've been in. I've been in there for hundreds, yes, hundreds of years. As an expression of my overwhelming gratitude I will grant you one wish.'

Tony Blair, being a world leader, knew exactly what to ask for. 'Peace in the Middle East!' he quickly replied.

The genie seemed confused. 'Middle East...Middle East... I can't seem to remember...can you help me out a little?'

The Prime Minister has a world map brought over and he carefully points out the affected area of the globe, recounting briefly the long-standing geopolitical instability of the area.

The genie's eyes widen and he says, 'Oh, yes. Now I remember. The Middle East! Whew. That's a tough one. You know, they've been fighting over there quite literally for millennia. I hate to admit it, but I think that's more than I can handle. I'm sorry. Can you wish for something else?'

Blair, obviously crestfallen at such a missed opportunity, can think of only one other wish: 'Could you make the British people like my wife?'

The genie pauses, grimaces, then says, 'Let me see that map again.'

Son: 'Dad, I have to do a special report for school. Can I ask you a question?'

Father: 'Sure son. What's the question?'

Son: 'What is politics?'

Father: 'Well, let's take our home for example. I am the wage earner, so let's call me 'Tony Blair'. Your mother is the administrator of money, so we'll call her 'Gordon Brown'. We take care of your needs, so we'll call you 'the People'. We'll call the maid 'The Working Class', and your baby brother we can call 'The Future'. Do you understand, Son?'

Son: 'I'm not really sure, Dad. I'll have to think about it'.

That night, awakened by his baby brother's crying, the boy went to see what was wrong. Discovering that the baby had seriously soiled his nappy, the boy went to his parents' room and found his mother sound asleep. He went to the maid's room where, peeking through the keyhole, he saw his father in bed with the maid. The boy's knocking went totally unheeded by his father and the maid, so the boy returned to his room and went back to sleep.

The next morning he reported to his father. 'Dad, now I think I understand what politics is.'

And the father said, 'Good son! Can you explain it to me in your own words?'

'Well dad, while Tony Blair is screwing the Working Class, Gordon Brown is sound asleep, the People are being completely ignored and the Future is full of shit,' came the reply.

A little boy wanted £100 badly and prayed for two weeks but nothing happened. Then he decided to write God a letter requesting the £100. When the post office received the letter to GOD, Heaven, they decided to send it to the Prime Minister, Tony Blair. The Prime Minister was so impressed, touched, and amused, that he told his chancellor Gordon Brown, to send the little boy a £5 note from Treasury funds. He thought this would appear to be a lot of money to a little boy.

The little boy was delighted with the £5 and sat down to write a thank you note to God which read: Dear God, thank you very much for sending me the money. However, I noticed that for some reason you had to send it through the Treasury and, as usual, those bastards deducted £95.

New Labour Viruses

Nick Brown Virus: your IBM suddenly claims it's a MAC.
Ron Davies Virus: sucks all the memory out of your computer.
Robin Cook Virus: makes a huge initial impact, then you forget it's there.
Margaret Beckett Virus: turns your hard disk into a 3.5 inch floppy.

Harriet Harman Virus: has no real function, but makes a pretty desktop.

Oona King Virus: expands your hard drive while putting too much pressure on your zip drive.

Boris Yeltsin, Bill Clinton and Peter Mandelson were invited to have dinner with God. During dinner He told them: 'I invited you here because I need three important people to send my message out to all people – tomorrow, I will destroy the earth.'

After dinner, Yeltsin immediately called together his Cabinet and told them: 'I have two very bad news items for you: 1. God really exists, and 2. Tomorrow He will destroy the earth.'

Clinton called an emergency meeting of the Senate and Congress and told them: 'I have good news and bad news: 1. The good news is: God really does exist. 2. The bad news is: tomorrow He's destroying the earth.'

Peter Mandelson reported back to Tony Blair and happily announced: 'I have two fantastic pieces of news. 1. I am one of three most important people on earth. 2. We won't have to open the Millenium Dome.

When Tony Blair was just a boy his mother prayed that Tony would grow up and become Prime Minister. So far, half of her prayers have been answered.

Q: Why is Harriet Harman like a laxative?
A: They both irritate the shit out of you.

Tony Benn and Ken Livingstone boarded a plane to Brussels. One sat in the window seat, the other in the middle seat. Just before take-off, Peter Mandelson appeared and took the aisle seat next to the Old Labour stalwarts. He kicked off his shoes, wiggled his toes and was settling in when Tony Benn, sitting in the window seat said,'I think I'll go up and get a mug of tea.'

'No problem,' said Mandelson,'I'll get it for you.' While he was away, Tony Benn picked up Mandelson's Armani shoe and spat in it. When the Prince of Darkness returned with the coke, Ken Livingstone looked up and remarked: 'That looks good. I think I'll have one too.'

Again, Mandelson obligingly went to fetch it. And while

he was gone, Livingstone picked up his other shoe and spat in it. Mandelson returned with the second mug of steaming hot tea and they all sat back and enjoyed the short flight to Brussels.

As the plane was landing Mandelson slipped his feet into his shoes and knew immediately what had happened. 'How long must this go on?' Mandelson asked, 'this enmity between Old Labour and New Labour people, this hatred, this animosity...this spitting in shoes and pissing in the tea.'

Q: How can you tell when a female New Labour MP reaches orgasm?
A: Her pager stops vibrating

Noel Gallagher, Peter Mandelson and Nicholas Fairbairn were sitting around in Heaven, bored out of their heavenly minds. Plucking up courage, they approach St Peter to ask if they might be given permission to return to Earth for a few short hours. St Peter isn't keen on the idea at all and tells them that if they even think of committing any sin they will go straight to Hell.

Zap! They find themselves in Soho. As they walk down Old Compton Street, Sir Nicholas Fairbairn sees a pub, but the moment he walks in, poof! he disappears. Mandelson and Gallagher look at each other and realize that St Peter was serious.

A moment later Noel Gallacher spies a packet of white powder lying in the street. He thinks for a moment and then bends to pick it up. Poof! Peter Mandelson disappears.

How To Talk About New Labour and Still Be Politically Correct

John Prescott does not have a beer gut,
He has developed a Liquid Grain Storage Facility.

Frank Dobson is not stupid,
He suffers from Minimal Cranial Development.

Neil Kinnock is not balding,
He is in Follicle Regression.

Robin Cook is not a cradle robber,
He prefers Generationally Differential Relationships.

Denzil Davies does not get falling-down drunk,
He becomes Accidentally Horizontal.

Gordon Brown does not have his head up his ass,
He suffers from Rectal-Cranial Inversion.

Ian McCartney is not short,
He is Anatomically Compact.

Fiona Mactaggart does not have a rich daddy,
She is a Recipient of Parental Asset Infusion.

John Prescott is not unsophisticated,
He is Socially Challenged.

John Prescott does not eat like a pig,
He suffers from Reverse Bulimia.

Janet Anderson does not undress you with her eyes,
She has an Introspective Pornographic Moment.

Robin Cook is not afraid of commitment,
He is Monogamously Challenged.

The European Union Commissioners have announced that agreement has been reached to adopt English as the preferred language for European communications, rather than German, which was the other possibility. As part of the negotiations, Her Majesty's Government conceded that English spelling has some room for improvement and has accepted a five-year phased plan for what will be known as Euro-English (Euro for short).

In the first year, 's' will be used instead of the soft 'c'. Sertainly , sivil servants will reseive this news with joy. Also, the hard 'c' will be replased with 'k'. Not only will this clear up konfusion, but typewriters kan have one less letter.

There will be glowing publik enthusiasm in the sekond year, when the troublesome 'ph' will be replaced by 'f'. This will make words like'fotograf' 20 per sent shorter.

In the third year, publik akseptanse of the new spelling kan be expekted to reach the stage where more komplikated changes are possible. Governments will enkorage the removal of double letters, which have always ben a deterent to akurate speling. Also, al wil agre that the horible mes of silent 's's in the languag is disgrasful, and they would go.

By the fourth year, peopl wil be reseptiv to steps such as replasing 'th' by 'z' and 'w' by 'v'.

During ze fifz year, ze unesesary 'o' kan be dropd from vords kontaining 'ou', and similar changes vud be aplid to ozer kombinations of leters.

After zis fifz year, ve vil hav a reli sensibl riten styl. Zer vil be no more trubls or difikultis and evrivun vil find it ezi tu understand ech ozer.

Ze drem vil finali kum tru.

L'Internationale – New Labour Version

The people's flag is salmon pink,
It's not as red as you might think.
White collar workers come and cheer
The Labour leader once a year.

So raise the umbrella high,
The bowler hat, the old school tie.
So people think we're still sincere,
We'll sing the Red Flag once a year.

L'Internationale – Revised Version

Arise, ye starveling Statisticians!
Arise, ye Bureaucratic Clerks!
Arise, Economists, Technicians,
And Synthesists of Ford and Marx!
Arise, all ye Government Inspectors,
Ye Co-Ordinators every man,
Trade Union Leaders and Directors,
For see, the World is yours to Plan!

World-planners, come rally;
The last fight let us face!
L'Internationale
Controls the human race!

At last imperfect competition
Shall yield to super-state cartels,
Research, collation, and prevision
By hand-picked academic swells.
United-Nations rehabilitation
And price-wage stabilizing pegs,
Combined with federalization,
Will set old Europe on its legs!

Then, experts, come rally,
The last Graph let us trace!
L'Internationale
Controls the human race!

We'll brave the free-consumers' rancour,
And all men's purchases arrange
Through Unitas or Keynesitas (or Bancour)
And a regulated world exchange.
Propensity to maximum consumption
Has been latent for a long time past
and with *our* administrative gumption
We'll make this round Globerich at last!

Then, expansionists, come rally,
The last loan let us place!
L'Internationale
Controls the Human Race!

Our scheduled schemes of reconstruction,
Our quotas, questionnaires, and doles,
Shall tap hot springs of wealth production
Under integrated world controls.
As in war we've evolved and fully tried rules
For mastering monopolies and mobs,
With out logarithmic charts and slide-rules
We now can all get cosmic jobs!

Then, bureaucrats, come rally;
The last chit let us chase!
L'Internationale
Controls the human race!

Q: What's the difference between a chorus line and the Labour Cabinet?
A: A chorus line has a cunning array of stunts.

Q: How do you change Frank Dobson's mind?
A: Blow in his ear.

A new young Labour MP is a little overwhelmed by his luxurious new Commons office. But with nothing in his In tray, he worries about what he should be doing. Suddenly he sees someone come into the outer office. Wanting to look busy, he picks up the phone and pretends to be talking to a senior government minister. He speaks loudly about government policy and his constituency. Finally he hangs up and asks the visitor: 'Can I help you?'

The man says: 'I've come to install the phone.'

New Labour Political Turn Ons

1 Tony Blair
2 Avocado dip
3 The chairs at Pont de la Tour
4 The grass on Hampstead Heath
5 John Prescott's love handles
6 Harriet Harman's hemline
7 Stephen Twigg's mane
8 Peter Mandelson's moustache
9 Tessa Jowell's pout
10 Dawn Primarolo's school mistress act

Q: Why did Tony and Cherie only have three children?
A: Because they heard that every fourth child born in the world is Chinese.

Q: What is the difference between Old Labour MPs and New Labour MPs?

A: Old Labour MPs wash their hands after going to the toilet. New Labour MPs don't piss on their hands in the first place.

Eighteen Examples of Blair Blah

Meaningless phrases with good alliteration and very few verbs. That's what Blair blah is all about. For those not familiar with the term, I first heard it used in Norfolk by a redoubtable lady called Marjorie Lloyd, who would listen attentively to a political speech and then dismiss it with the words: 'Doesn't mean a thing – it's all blah!' Tony Blair's skill is that he mixes blah with substance. But he does have a tendency to overdo it, play to the crowd. New Labour New Britain. Britain United. One Nation. New Labour. See what I mean?

1. The power of all for the good of each
2. Ours is a passion allied to reason
3. A thousand days for a thousand years
4. Labour's coming home

5. Tough on crime – tough on the causes of crime
6. Saying what we mean, meaning what we say
7. A hand up, not a hand out
8. Longtermism in action
9. Education, Education, Education
10. Call me Tony
11. The settlement train is leaving
12. Marching in step to a General Election
13. Fairness, not favours
14. Education is liberty
15. Nation of all the talents
16. Leadership not drift
17. For the many not the few
18. For the future, not the past

Q: What do you get when you cross a New Labour MP with a prostitute?
A: A fucking know-it-all.

In the beginning was the Plan

And then came the Assumptions

And the Assumptions were without form

And the Plan was without substance

And darkness was on the face of the workers

And they spoke amongst themselves, saying, 'It is a crock of shit, and it stinketh.'

And the workers went unto their trade unions officials and said, 'It is a pail of dung, and none may abide the odour thereof.'

And the trade union officials went to their Labour councillor saying, 'It is a container of excrement, and it is very strong, such that none may abide by it.'

And the Labour councillor went to the local Labour MP, saying, 'It is a vessel of fertilizer and none may abide its strength.'

And the Labour MP went to the Cabinet Minister, saying, 'It contains that which aids plant growth, and it is very powerful.'

And the Cabinet Minister went to the Tony Blair and said
unto him, 'This new plan will actively promote the
growth and vigour of the economy with powerful
effects.'
And the Prime Minister looked upon the Plan and say that
it was good.
And the Plan became official Labour Party policy.
This is how Shit happens.

David Blunkett was waiting to cross the road when his
guide dog peed on his leg. He reached into his pocket, took
out a biscuit and gave it to the dog. A passerby who had
seen the entire incident was very touched. 'That's very
tolerant of you after what he just did.'

'Not really,' replied Blunkett. 'I'm just finding out where
his mouth is so I can kick him in the nuts.'

Q: Why doesn't Clare Short wear skirts?
A: Because her balls would show.

Q: What are the two worst things about Robin Cook?
A: His face.

Q: What's the difference between Margaret Beckett and the rear end of a horse?
A: I don't know either.

Q: How many Alastair Campbells does it take to screw in a light bulb?
A: None of your fucking business.

Q: How many Old Labour MPs does it take to change a light bulb?
A: What do you mean change? It's a perfectly good light bulb. We've had it for 100 years and it's worked just fine.

Q: How many Frank Dobsons does it take to change a lightbulb?
A: One, but it has to be a pretty dim bulb.

Q: How many Gordon Browns does it take to screw in a light bulb?
A: Two. One to screw it in and one to send the bill to the next generation.

Tony Blair's Worst Nightmares

1. Answering the phone and hearing 'Hi Tone, it's the Scouse Git here'
2. Waking up and finding 1 May 1997 was an April Fool's joke – one month late
3. At one of his 'Talk to Tony' meetings the whole audience consists of Jeremy Paxman
4. Running out of Chianti
5. Forgetting the word 'new'
6. Something involving Prescott and a sheep
7. Neil Kinnock makes speech hinting at return to British politics
8. John Smith makes surprise guest appearance on *X-Files*
9. The Italian government makes him pay for his holiday
10. Cherie is made redundant

Having hailed a taxi, Frank Dobson was enjoying the view when the taxi driver interrupted his thoughts by yelling: 'Oi mate, have you heard the latest Frank Dobson joke?'

Baffled, Frank spluttered: 'But I am Frank Dobson'.

'In that case,' replied the cabbie, 'I'll tell it very slowly.'

Q: How do you get a Labour MP to do sit-ups?
A: Glue his pager between his ankles…

Tony Blair is visiting a school. In one class, he asks the students if anyone can give him an example of a 'tragedy'. One little boy stands up and offers that, 'if my best friend who lives next door was playing in the street and a car came along and killed him, that would be a tragedy.'

'No,' the Prime Minister says, 'that would be an Accident.'

A girl raises her hand. 'If a school bus carrying 50 children drove off a cliff, killing everyone involved ... that would be a tragedy'.

'I'm afraid not, 'explains Tony, 'that is what we would call a Great Loss.'

The room is silent, none of the other children volunteer. 'What?' asks Blair. 'Isn't there any one here who can give me an example of a tragedy?'

Finally, a boy in the back raises his hand. In a timid voice, he says: 'If an airplane carrying Tony Blair was blown up by a bomb, THAT would be a tragedy.'

'Wonderful!' beams the Prime Minister. 'Marvellous! And can you tell me WHY that would be a tragedy?'

'Well,' says the boy, 'because it wouldn't be an accident, and it certainly wouldn't be a great loss!'

Economic and Political Theory 101 with Cows

`Feudalism:` you have two cows. Your lord takes some of the milk.

Pure Socialism: you have two cows. The government takes them and puts them in a barn with everyone else's cows. You have to take care of all the cows. The government gives you as much milk as you need.

Bureaucratic Socialism: you have two cows. The government takes them and puts them in a barn with everyone else's cows. They are cared for by ex-chicken farmers.

You have to take care of the chickens the government took from the chicken farmers. The government gives you as much milk and eggs the regulations say you should need.

Fascism: you have two cows. The government takes both, hires you to take care of them, and sells you the milk.

Pure Communism: you have two cows. Your neighbours help you take care of them, and you all share the milk.

Russian Communism: You have two cows. You have to take care of them, but the government takes all the milk.

Cambodian Communism: you have two cows. The government takes both and shoots you.

Dictatorship: you have two cows. The government takes both and drafts you.

Totalitarianism: your have two cows. The government takes them and denies they ever existed. Milk is banned.

Pure Democracy: you have two cows. Your neighbours decide who gets the milk.

Representative Democracy: you have two cows. Your neighbours pick someone through a vote to tell you who gets the milk.

Singaporean Democracy: you have two cows. The government fines you for illegally keeping two unlicensed farm animals in an apartment.

American Democracy: the government promises to give you two cows if you vote for it. After the election, the president is impeached for speculating in cow futures. The press dubs the affair 'Cowgate'.

British Democracy: you have two cows. You feed them sheep's brains and they go mad. The government doesn't do anything.

Bureaucracy: you have two cows. At first the government regulates what you can feed them and when you can milk them. Then it pays you not to milk them. Then it takes both, shoots one, milks the other and pours the milk down the drain. Then it requires you to fill out forms accounting for the missing cows.

Capitalism: you have two cows. You sell one and buy a bull which you use to breed the other cow as well as every other cow in the area. Then you start exporting sperm from the

bull to emerging markets. After several years of expansion, your company floats on the stock exchange. The SIB eventually intends legal proceedings against you and your spouse for insider trading. After a lengthy court battle, you are found guilty and sentenced to ten years in prison, of which you actually serve seven weeks. When you come out of prison, you buy two chickens. Then…

Hong Kong Capitalism: you have two cows. You sell three of them to your publicly listed company, using letters of credit opened by your brother-in-law at the bank, then execute a debt/equity swap with an associated general offer so that you get all four cows back, with a tax deduction for keeping five cows. The milk rights of six cows are transferred via a Panamanian intermediary to a Cayman Islands company secretly owned by the majority shareholder, who sells the rights to all seven cows' milk back to the listed company and proceeds from the sale are deferred. The annual report says that the company owns eight cows, with an option on one more. Meanwhile, you kill the two cows because the feng shui is bad.

Environmentalism: you have two cows. The government bans you from milking or killing them.

Feminism: you have two cows. They get married and adopt a veal calf.

Political Correctness: you are associated with (the concept of 'ownership' is a symbol of the phallo-centric, war-

mongerism, intolerant past) two differently aged (but no less valuable to society) bovines of unspecified gender.

Counter Culture: wow, dig it, like there's these two cows, man, grazing in the hemp field. You got to have some of this milk!

Botulism: you have two cows. They get into spoiled grain...

Pure Anarchy: you have two cows. Either you sell the milk at a fair price or your neighbours try to take the cows and kill you.

Libertarianism: whatever...

Surrealism: you have two giraffes. The government requires you to take harmonica lessons. The sun rises in the north on alternate Tuesdays.

New Labour: you have New Cows. New Cows New Britain. Our Mission New Cows. New Britain. New Cows New Britain.

Cherie Blair, Pauline Prescott and Mo Mowlam attend the World Women's Conference. Cherie was invited to speak first: 'At last year's conference we spoke about being more assertive with our husbands. Well, after the conference I went home and told Tony that I would no longer cook for him and that he would have to do it himself. After the first day I saw nothing. After the second day I saw nothing. But after the third day I saw that he had cooked a wonderful roast lamb.' The crowd cheered.

Later, Mo Mowlam stood up: 'After last year's conference I went home and told my husband that I would no longer do his laundry and that he would have to do it himself. After the first day I saw nothing. After the second day I saw nothing. But after the third day I saw that he had done not only his own washing but my washing as well.' The crowd cheered.

Next, Pauline Prescott rose to her feet: 'After last year's conference I went home and told my husband that I would no longer do his shopping and that he would have to do it himself. After the first day I saw nothing. After the second day I saw nothing. But after the third day I could see a little bit out of my left eye.'

One day, while Tony Blair is out jogging round St James's Park he sees a little boy looking into a cardboard box and says, 'Hey kid, what's in the box ?'

The kid says, 'My dog just had puppies.'

Blair asks him what kind of dogs they are.

'These are New Labour puppies,' answers the kid.

The next day Tony and Cherie are out walking and come upon the same kid. Blair grins in the way only he knows how and says, 'Hey kid, tell my wife what kind of puppies you done got there.'

The kid says.' Conservative puppies'.

Blair is somewhat embarrassed and confused, says, 'But kid, yesterday you told me that them there were New Labour puppies.'

'That's right. But last night they opened their eyes.'

You Might Be New Labour If...

1. You think 'proletariat' is a type of cheese.
2. You've named your kids 'Mandy' or 'Alastair'
3. You've tried to argue that poverty could be abolished if people were just allowed to keep more of their minimum wage
4. You've ever tried to prove Jesus was a socialist and would have been in favour of the welfare state
5. You're pro abortion but anti the death penalty
6. You've ever uttered the phrase, 'Why don't we just bomb the sons of bitches'
7. You scream 'Tough on crime' while making love
8. When people say 'Marx', you think 'Groucho'
9. Welfare to Work makes a lot of sense to you
10. You wonder if donations to Childline are tax-deductable
11. You came of age in the 1960s and don't remember Bob Dylan
12. You confuse Lenin with Lennon
13. You think John Humphrys represents media impartiality
14. You've ever given money to a tramp so he can buy more, er...food
15. You pay a 185 per cent markup for organically grown food
16. You hate petits pois but you just love mange touts

Issue	New Labour	Conservative
Criminals	Give them a second chance	Give them the swift sword of death
The Poor	Give them some food	Give them the swift sword of death
Endangered Species	Give them protection	Give them the swift sword of death
Dictators	Give them a way out	Give them the swift sword of death
The Unemployed	Give them a job	Give them the swift sword of death
The Cost	£7,000,000,000,000	£29.99 (cost of one sword)

A parliamentary candidate was canvassing in his constituency when he came across a fierce dog in the garden of a house he wished to visit. A woman could be seen in the upstairs window of the house.

The candidate asked the woman if her dog was savage, she answered no.

As he entered the garden he was promptly savaged by the dog.

'I thought you said your dog wasn't savage,' said the candidate, feeling somewhat aggrieved.

'She isn't,' said the woman with an air that said the candidate was obviously a fool, 'that isn't my dog.'

Twenty Six Things You Didn't Know About Tony Blair

(courtesy of Matthew Parris)

1. He has terrible teeth
2. He looks like a vampire
3. It is not true that Tony Blair is attractive to women. He's too pretty. He's a man's idea of a man who attracts women. Seven out of nine women in the Westminster Press Gallery do not fancy Tony Blair. Gordon Brown scores four.
4. He went to public school
5. He went to Oxford

6. His Dad became a Tory
7. He smiles too much
8. He cannot possibly be as nice as he seems. All politicians must rise through a nasty political process, work with nasty people in nasty parties and prosper. He has. He must be pretending to be nice
9. He cannot lack a simple ambition for office as he claims. He must be lying
10. He spends too much time on his hair
11. He looks like a prototype for something, but nobody is sure what
12. Nobody had heard of him before 1992
13. He may be a Vulcan. This man is too good to be true. I believe that military strategists on the planet Vulcan, having infiltrated into Westminster an early attempt at an Earthling politician, John Redwood, have now learnt from the mistakes in this design. They have sent an improved version with added charm. He has pointed ears
14. He probably approves of Cliff Richard
15. He may be Cliff Richard
16. The Tories will say he's a boy sent to do a man's job
17. Richard Littlejohn supports him
18. He used to wear flares
19. He was almost certainly a fan of Peter, Paul and Mary, the New Seekers, the Carpenters, Bucks Fizz, Abba…
20. He probably listens to Classic FM now

21. His father was a lawyer
22. He could just as well have been the leader of the Conservative Party or the SDP or the Liberal Party or the Green Party or Archbishop of Canterbury or a progressive missionary, or in charge of Bob Geldof's PR, or director of a major charity, or chairman of English Heritage, or General Secretary of a small, service sector trade union, or a management consultant, or King Herod, or the leader if the Dutch Social Democrats, or manager of a small plastics factory in Enfield where he is also sidesman in the local church and takes his daughters to pony classes in a newish Volvo
23. He wears pastel suits
24. He reminds us of Bill Clinton
25. If he had ever smoked maijuana he would *not* have inhaled
26. He doesn't fool me

Q: Why did the post office have to cancel the Tony Blair postage stamp?
A: People kept spitting on the wrong side of the stamp.

Two friends are discussing politics on Election Day, each trying to no avail to persuade the other to switch sides.

Finally, one says to the other: 'Look, it's clear that we are unalterably opposed on every political issue. Our votes will surely cancel out. Why not save ourselves some time and both agree to not vote today?'

The other agrees enthusiastically and they part.

Shortly after that, a friend of the first one who had heard the conversation says, 'That was a sporting offer you made.'

'Not really,' says the second. This is the third time I've done this today. '

It so happens that the Pope and Robin Cook died at the same time. There was a mix-up, and the Pope was sent to Hell and Cook went to Heaven. Of course, Satan immediately realized the error. He was quite displeased, so he set about to rectify the situation at once. Nevertheless, relations between Heaven and Hell being what they are, it took a full day for the trade to be arranged. When the Pope heard he was going to Heaven after all, he was much relieved, but being the caring soul he was, he was worried that Robin would be upset at the change. So when they met halfway, the Pope said, 'Mr Cook, I know you must be very disappointed, but you know I did live 80 years of a clean life bound to God, so that I could claim my reward and kneel at the feet of the Virgin.'

And Cook, grinning, replies, 'Well, Your Holiness, I'm afraid you're a little too late for that!'

Q: Who were the first Communists?

A: Adam and Eve. They had no clothes, no apartment, only one apple between them, and thought they lived in Paradise.

Tony Blair goes on a peace-seeking mission to Iraq and to meet Saddam Hussein. The meeting goes well and they retire for dinner. The conversation turns to personal matters. 'Do you have a hobby?' asks the Iraqi dictator.

Tony Blair thinks for a second and replies: 'Yes, I collect jokes that people tell about me.'

Curious to know more about Saddam's habits, Blair proceeds to ask if he too has a hobby. 'Yes,' replies Saddam, 'I collect people who tell jokes about me.'

Geoffrey Robinson was forced to travel by train for the first time in many years when his Rolls was involved in an accident. However, he welcomed this chance to have some contact with 'ordinary people'. As he passed through the station he said to the man who punched his ticket, 'How long have you been doing this?'

'Oh,' said the ticket collector, 'nearly thirty years.'

The former Paymaster General studied his ticket carefully. 'You do it very well,' he said.

A man was arrested after running along Whitehall shouting 'Tony Blair is an evil dictator' at the top of his voice. He was given three years in prison. One for defamation and two for revealing state secrets.

Tony Blair slips on the wet floor after getting out of his bath. 'Mon Dieu,' exclaims Cherie. The Prime Minister gets up from the bathroom floor slowly and says: 'How many times do I have to tell you, Cherie. At home, you may call me Tony.'

Tony Blair is running late for his next meeting when his Private Secretary comes into the room and says that he has two visitors waiting. 'Who are they?' demands the Prime Minister.

'The Archbishop of Canterbury and Gordon Brown,' replies the aide.

'Show the Archbishop in first,' says Blair. 'At least I only have to kiss his hand.'

Top Ten Ways of Spotting a Bleeding Heart Liberal

1 You go pink with rage at the thought of paedophiles being executed, but defend the killing of unborn children as an expression of choice
2 You believe animals can think, trees have feelings and the foetus is a blob of protoplasm
3 You don't believe in marriage, except for homosexuals
4 You are quite happy to legalize drugs and outlaw handguns
5 You are permanently 'worried' about things and you use the word 'community' a lot
6 You don't think Gerry Adams is all bad
7 You think the rehabilitation of criminals is more important than punishing them
8 You think that whatever their level, taxes should be increased
9 Gordon Brown's neoindigenous growth theory turns you on
10 You don't understand people who are against positive discrimination and are more than happy to sacrifice someone else's job to assuage your own guilt

Ever one for forward planning, Tony Blair makes some inquiries at his local cemetery about reserving a plot for when his time comes. The clerk told him: 'The price is £500. That may sound a lot but you won't be disturbed for over 200 years.'

Blair made some rapid calculations on the back of an envelope. 'I'll give you five pence,' he says. 'After all, I'll only need it for three days.'

Twin boys are sent home from school with a note saying:

'Dear Mrs Smith, your boys say their names are Blair and Brown. Is this true or are they making fun of me?'

Mrs Smith replies:

'Dear teacher, the name is Miss Smith, not Mrs Smith, and if you had two little bastards, what would you call them?'

There are six people on a plane: the pilot, John Prescott, Tony Blair and Gordon Brown, a priest and a young man. When something goes wrong with the plane the pilot announces he is taking one of the five parachutes on board and they must decide among themselves who will take the remaining four.

John Prescott declares that as he is the voice of the working man and that Labour won't get re-elected without him, he must jump and, taking a parachute, jumps out of the plane.

Tony Blair says that as Prime Minister he is the person the whole country looks up to and without him the Government would collapse. He too takes a parachute and jumps. Then Gordon Brown gets up. 'I am the best educated and most intelligent Chancellor of the Exchequer this century. I must jump.' He too jumps out of the plane.

Then the priest rises and says to the young man. 'My son, I am old and have lived my time, take the last parachute and jump.'

But the young man protests: 'Father, hurry up – there are two parachutes left, one for each of us. Put on one of them and jump.'

'But how is that?' asks the priest.

'That guy who said he is educated and intelligent – he took my sleeping bag.'

Q: Why do Labour governments resemble a violin?
A: Because they are held on the left but played on the right.

A New Labour MP goes for a haircut wearing Walkman-style earphones. The MP refuses to remove the earphones and insists that the hairdresser should work around them. The effect of the haircut is so soothing that the MP soon falls fast asleep. Seeing this, the hairdresser quietly removes the headphones to make cutting the MPs hair a little easier. After a couple of minutes, the MP slumps forward, dead. Shocked, the hairdresser picks up the earphones to hear what the MP had been listening to. Out of the earphones comes the distinctive voice of Peter Mandelson: 'Breathe in…Breathe out…Breathe in…Breathe out.'

Tony Blair goes into the men's room at Parliament, and finds John Major already inside at a urinal. Blair steps up to the urinal beside Major's.

When Major spots Blair, he hurriedly zips up. Blair says to Major, 'What's your hurry, John? Didn't you want me to see?'

Major says, 'I most certainly didn't want you to see; because every time you see something big, working well, and privately held, you want to tax it.'

Conservatives in recent years have stepped up their campaign efforts in Labour districts. A Conservative campaigner makes a strong attempt to persuade a Labour voter to vote Conservative, but the voter won't budge.

'My grandfather was Labour, my father was Labour, and I'm Labour,' the voter says. The Conservative tries to defeat him with logic, asking, 'If your grandfather was a thief, and your father was a thief, would you be a thief?'

The Labour voter thinks about that a moment, and finally replies, 'No. Then I'd be a Conservative.'

A junior Labour MP with political ambitions loses his pet parrot. He looks everywhere, all around the neighbourhood, in the park, everywhere. He can't find the parrot. Finally he goes around to Millbank, and tells Alastair Campbell his problem.

Campbell is a little puzzled. 'Look, I'm sorry you lost your bird, but this is New Labour, we're about saving education, not finding lost pets.'

'Oh, I know that', says the Labour MP. 'I just wanted you to know, if you find my parrot – I don't know where he could have picked up all his political ideas.'

Q. What was John Prescott worried about laughing at a comedy show?
A. He heard that dicks throw up when they're excited.

Q. What do you call a group of Labour Cabinet Ministers in a circle?
A. A dope ring.

Q: What does John Prescott have TGIF on his shoes for?
A: Just to remind him that toes go in first.

Clare Short couldn't attend a dinner in London which Robin Cook and Gordon Brown had been to. Clare asked Robin, 'was the food good?'
Robin said, 'Yes, I had 6 potatoes, 4 slices of roast beef, 28 slices of carrot and 481 peas.'

Clare said, 'Liar, you can't possibly have counted them!'

'But what else could we do while listening to Gordon's speech?'

Robin Cook, a politician rarely accused of being any less than 100 per cent vain was at an EU Foreign Ministers' dinner and, having droned on for half an hour about himself and how brilliant he was at his job, turned to his dining companion and said: 'I have talked about myself for long enough. Let's talk about you. What do you think of me?'

A Conservative MP, out for his mid-afternoon constitutional in St James's Park is horrified to see someone lying face down on the pathway. It is clear that the poor unfortunate needs some medical attention. 'Hang on a second,' he says, 'I'll go and call an ambulance.'

A few minutes later a New Labour MP comes along and views the scene with some concern. 'Good gracious,' he says with alarm. 'The person who did this to you really needs help. If only I knew who it was.'

Presently, a Liberal Democrat MP happens on the scene, having spent an hour with one of his focus groups. Bending down on one knee, he whispers to the prostrate figure, 'Tell me, what did the others say?'

A left-wing delegate at the Labour Party Conference is at a busy fringe meeting and suddenly spots someone across the room who he hasn't seen for years. Eventually he makes his way through the crowds and says: 'Well, well, well, you have changed, Arthur. You've gone grey, lost weight, shaved off your moustache and even got contact lenses. Arthur Reid, I never thought the Millbank image-makers would get to you!'

The man replied: 'But my name isn't Arthur Reid, it's Darren Van Hansen.'

'Absolutely astonishing,' the left winger replied. 'They've even got you to change your name!'

Seen on a calendar:

'The halcyon days of parliamentary government were those when the Chancellor of the Exchequer lived within his income and not mine.'

Peter Mandelson had only been in the Cabinet for a few weeks when he began to think that he wasn't being paid the going rate for the job. After all, even a Cabinet Minister has bills to pay. He decided to go and see the Prime Minister and ask for a rise. 'What!' exclaimed Tony, 'you've only been in the Cabinet for five minutes. I believe in performance-related pay. In my Government, to get more money, you must work yourself up.'

'I have! I have!' insisted Mandy indignantly. 'Look at me – I'm trembling all over.'

A pretty young college graduate thought she had secured the job of her dreams – assistant private secretary to an ageing New Labour Cabinet Minister. She found that she had to travel a lot with him on business but was dismayed when he insisted on acting as if she were his girlfriend. Whenever they ate in a restaurant, he would call her 'darling' or 'dear' in front of the waiters.

At first she was patient, hoping that he would grow tired of it. But then, as they were entering an especially high-class restaurant she decided to take action. As the Head Waiter approached to seat them, the Secretary of State asked her: 'Where would you like to sit, sweetheart?'

'Anywhere you like, Daddy,' the girl replied.

A New Labour MP was complaining to one of her Conservative colleagues about how hard she had to work and how this had affected her social life.

'I also had have that problem,' said the Conservative, who had been an MP for a little longer, 'but I came up with a very simple solution.'

'What's that?' asked the Labour MP eagerly.

'The secret is working only half days.'

'Only half days!' exclaimed the Labour MP. 'That's amazing!'

'And the best thing,' her colleague continued, 'is that it doesn't matter which 12 hours you work.'

Twenty Great New Labour Lies

1 I have nothing to hide
2 I challenge the press to follow me and see
3 I know nothing about it
4 I knew nothing about it
5 I knew a little about it
6 It's only a rumour
7 There is no plot
8 There is no conspiracy
9 I was only obeying orders
10 I was only doing my job
11 It was in the public interest
12 I'll prove my innocence
13 There is no cause for concern
14 There is light at the end of the tunnel
15 Your taxes have not gone up
16 It's a matter of principle

17 We're doing our best
18 We all want to see this sorted out
19 Tony Benn is a valued colleague
20 There is nothing wrong with my mortgage application

A Labour Club in the North East hasn't been persuaded of the merits of New Labour. Spotted recently on the noticeboard: 'It should be a matter of common courtesy but some women still fail to *lift* the seat when they have finished. In future ladies, will you kindly oblige.'

Q: How do you make David Blunkett's dog go woof?
A: Douse it in petrol and throw a match at it.

Q: What is Ron Davies's favourite bird?
A: The woodpecker

Tony Blair and Robin Cook are flying to Washington to visit Bill Clinton. Suddenly the engine fails and the plane begins to plunge into the sea. 'Quick,' shouts the Prime Minister, 'grab a parachute and jump'.

Cook blinks, looks around him and says: 'What about the secretaries?'

Blair stares at him incredulously and screams, 'Fuck the secretaries!'

Cook pauses for a moment, then asks: 'Do you think we have time?'

Q: What's the difference between an incoherent John Prescott speech and a coherent John Prescott speech?
A: About ten pints.

Q: What's the difference between Stephen Byers and a shower?
A: A shower has to be turned on before it's wet.

Q: Why does Frank Dobson wear earmuffs?
A: To cut down the draft.

Q: What do Peter Mandelson and a freezer have in common?
A. They both have ice on the inside.

Q: Why do politicians masturbate?
A: So they can have sex with the only person they love.

Q: What do you call a handcuffed Cabinet Minister?
A: Trustworthy.

New Labour Spin: 7% unemployment is acceptable to 93% of the population.

When politicians want your opinion, they'll give it to you.

Q: What's red, yellow and brown and looks good on an MP?
A: A tumour

'Will you even forget that lovely weekend we had together on the French Riviera,' the MP asked his secretary.
　'What's it worth,' came the reply.

The MP's secretary breezed in one morning and told her boss: 'I've got some good news and some bad news.'

'Look,' replied the MP, 'I'm very busy this morning so cut the cackle and spit it out.'

'Well,' she replied, 'the good news is you're not sterile…'

Flip-Flops

All politicians change their minds. Some are more honest about it than others. Margaret Thatcher would deny until she was blue in the face that she had ever done a U turn on any policy. In order to become electable, New Labour have had to perform some political acrobatics which make the term U turn almost an understatement. So what? If you change your mind and come up with the right answer, it doesn't really matter how much your opponents chide you for it. The term 'flip-flop', apart from being a less than fetching form of footwear has also entered the political vocabulary in America. It was used to good effect by the Republicans against Bill Clinton in a TV advert which demonstrated how many times Bill Clinton has changed his policies in his first term as President. Roll the film…

PROMINENT CABINET MEMBERS REFRESH THEIR MEMORIES

Flip: 'Without an active, interventionist industrial policy… Britain faces the future of having to compete on dangerously unequal terms.' *The Times*, 19 May 1988.

Flop: 'New Labour does not believe it is the job of government to interfere in the running of business.' Speech to the Nottingham Chamber of Commerce, 19 January 1996.

Flip: 'I am absolutely committed to the goal of full employment.' Speech to Labour Party Conference, October 1994.

Flop: 'There is no longer such a thing as a job for life. Long-term structural unemployment has become a fact of life.' Speech in Cape Town, 14 October 1996.

Flip: 'We'll create two million jobs in five years.' 1983 Election address.

Flop: 'I don't actually favour putting targets on it [full employment].' BBC TV, 12 June 1994.

Flip: 'I agree entirely that if you set it [the minimum wage] too high it will have an adverse impact on the jobs market.' BBC TV Money Programme, 24 September 1995.

Flop: 'I have not accepted that the minimum wage will cost jobs…I have simply accepted that econometric models indicate a potential jobs impact.' Letter to the *Independent*.

Flip: 'Most people would accept that an employer gains if a trade union is weakened. The proposed form of electoral procedure imposed and enforced upon every trade union will enmesh trade unions in legal battles and cause them administrative obstacles. That will weaken their ability to pursue the industrial interest of their members.' *Hansard*, 26 March 1984.

Flop: 'We are not going back to the old battles. You have heard me say this many times: I will say it again. There is not going to be a repeal of all Tory trade union laws. It is not what the members want – it is not what the country wants.' Speech to the TUC, 12 September 1995.

Flip: 'Under my leadership I will never allow this country to

be isolated or left behind in Europe.' Speech to Labour Party Conference, 4 October 1994.

Flop: 'If it is in Britain's interests to be isolated through the use of the national veto, then we will be isolated.' (Source to follow.)

Flip: 'We'll negotiate a withdrawal from the EEC which has drained our natural resources and destroyed jobs.' Election address in the 1983 General Election.

Flop: 'I always believed that it was important for Britain to be in Europe.' December 1994.

Flip: 'Having fought long and hard for [their freedoms, unions] will not give them up lightly. We shall oppose the Bill which is a scandalous and undemocratic measure against the trade union movement.' Speaking on the Trade Union Bill, November 1983.

Flop: 'The basic elements of that legislation: ballots before strikes, for union elections [and] restrictions on mass picketing are here to stay.' November 1994.

Flip: 'Parliamentary Labour CND supports the removal of all nuclear weapons from British territory and expresses its solidarity with all campaigners for peace.' Text of a newspaper advert in *Sanity* signed by Tony Blair in May 1986.

Flop: 'Labour will retain Britain's nuclear capability, with the number of warheads no greater than the present total.' April 1992.

Flip: 'Labour is committed to a regional assembly for Wales and to regional assembles for England.' June 1994
Flop: 'There is not a consensus about regional assemblies in England...We are not committed to regional assemblies in England.' March 1995

Warranty Card on Purchased Member of Parliament

Dear Special Interest,
Congratulations on the purchase of your genuine Member of Parliament. With regular maintenance your Member of Parliament should provide you with a lifetime of sweetheart deals, insider information, preferential legislation and other fine services. Before you begin using your product, we would appreciate it if you would take the time to fill out this customer service card. This information will not be sold to any other party, and will be used solely to aid us in better fulfilling your future needs in political influence.

1 Which of our fine products did you buy?
- ❏ Prime Minister
- ❏ Cabinet Minister
- ❏ Backbencher

2 How did you hear about your Member of Parliament?
- ❏ Please check all that apply.
- ❏ TV ad
- ❏ Magazine/newspaper ad
- ❏ Shared jail cell with
- ❏ Former law partner of
- ❏ Unindicted co-conspirator with
- ❏ Islington crony of
- ❏ Procured for
- ❏ Related to
- ❏ Recommended by lobbyist
- ❏ Recommended by organized-crime figure
- ❏ Frequently mentioned in conspiracy theories
- ❏ Solicited bribe from me
- ❏ Attempted to seduce me

3. How do you expect to use your Member of Parliament?
- ❏ Obtain lucrative government contracts
- ❏ Have my prejudices turned into law
- ❏ Obtain diplomatic concessions
- ❏ Obtain trade concessions
- ❏ Have embargo lifted from own nation/ally

87

- ❏ Have embargo imposed on enemy/rival nation/religious infidels
- ❏ Obtain patronage job for self/spouse/mistress
- ❏ Forestall military action against self/allies
- ❏ Instigate military action against internal enemies/aggressors/targets for future conquest
- ❏ Impede criminal/ civil investigation of self/associates/spouse
- ❏ Obtain pardon for self/associates/spouse
- ❏ Inflict punitive legislation on class enemies/rivals/hated ethnic groups
- ❏ Inflict punitive regulation on business competitors/environmental exploiters/capitalist pigs

4. What factors influenced your purchase?
- ❏ Performance of currently owned model
- ❏ Reputation
- ❏ Price
- ❏ Appearance
- ❏ Party affiliation
- ❏ Professed beliefs of Member of Parliament
- ❏ Actual beliefs of Member of Parliament
- ❏ Orders from boss/superior officer/foreign government
- ❏ Blackmail
- ❏ Celebrity endorsement

5. Is this product intended as a replacement for a currently owned Member of Parliament?

❏ Yes/No
❏ If you answered 'yes,' please indicate your reason(s) for changing models.
❏ Excessive operating/maintenance costs
❏ Needs have grown beyond capacity of current model
❏ Defect in current model
❏ Dead
❏ Senile
❏ Indicted
❏ Convicted
❏ Resigned in disgrace
❏ Switched parties/beliefs
❏ Outbribed by competing interest

Thank you for your valuable time. Always remember: in choosing a Member of Parliament you have chosen the best politician that money can buy.

New Labour-Speak: a Translation

1 Metabolically challenged: dead
2 Cerebrally challenged: stupid
3 Chronologically gifted: old
4 Client of the correctional system: prisoner
5 Economically marginalized: poor
6 Follicularly challenged: bald
7 Melanin-impoverished: white
8 Motivationally dispossessed: lazy
9 Person of substance: fat person
10 Vehicle-appearance specialist: car washer
11 Street activity index: crime rate
12 Fiscally challenged institution: bankrupt savings and loan
13 Residentially challenged: homeless
14 Aesthetically challenged: ugly
15 Geological correction: earthquake

Tony Blair's New Year's Resolutions

1 Take more notice of that Harman woman's ass
2 Not to worry about the hair loss – no, really
3 To use more verbs
4 Occasionally to disagree with Peter Mandelson
5 To ditch that plank Dobson
6 Tell people to 'Call me Anthony'
7 Improve approval ratings to 110 per cent
8 Hand William Hague a baby's dummy at PM's Question Time and tell him to 'Go suck on it'
9 Do something about the Ford Galaxy
10 Buy some new brown paper bags – if you get my meaning

Stephen Byers, upset that people keep ignoring him, goes to see his psychiatrist.

'Doc,' he said, I have this problem, people keep ignoring me!

The doctor said, 'Next please!'

It was getting a little crowded in Heaven, so God decided to change the admittance policy. The new law was that, in order to get into Heaven, you had to have a really bummer day on the day that you died. The policy would go into effect at noon the next day.

So, the next day at 12.01, the first person came to the gates of Heaven.

The Angel at the gate, remembering the new policy, promptly asked the man, 'Before I let you in, I need you to tell me how your day was going when you died.'

'No problem,' the man said. 'I came home to my 25th floor apartment on my lunch hour and caught my wife having an affair. But her lover was nowhere in sight; immediately I began searching for him. My wife was half naked and yelling at me as I searched the entire apartment.

'Just as I was about to give up, I happened to glance out onto the balcony and noticed that there was a man hanging off the edge by his fingertips! The nerve of that guy! Well, I ran out onto the balcony and stomped on his fingers until he fell to the ground. But wouldn't you know it, he landed in some trees and bushes that broke his fall and he didn't die.

This ticked me off even more. In a rage, I went back inside to get the first thing I could get my hands on to throw at him. Oddly enough, the first thing I thought of was the refrigerator. I unplugged it, pushed it out onto the balcony, and tipped it over the side. It plummeted 25

storeys and crushed him. The excitement of the moment was so great that I had a heart attack and died almost instantly.'

The Angel sat back and thought a moment. Technically, the guy did have a bad day. It was a crime of passion. So, the Angel announces, 'OK, sir. Welcome to the kingdom of Heaven,' and let him in.

A few seconds later the next guy came up. To the Angel's surprise, it was Gordon Brown. 'Mr Brown, before I can let you in, I need to hear about what your day was like when you died.'

Mr Brown said, 'No problem. But you're not going to believe this, I was on the balcony of my 26th floor apartment doing my daily exercises. I had been under a lot of pressure so I was really pushing hard to relieve my stress. I guess I got a little carried away, slipped, and accidentally fell over the side. Luckily, I was able to catch myself by my fingertips on the balcony below mine. But all of a sudden this crazy man comes out of his apartment, starts cussing, and stomps on my fingers.

'Well, of course I fell. I hit some trees and bushes at the bottom which broke my fall so I didn't die right away. As I'm lying there face up on the ground, unable to move and in excruciating pain, I see this guy push his refrigerator of all things off the balcony. It falls the 25 floors and lands on top of me killing me instantly. '

The Angel is quietly laughing to himself as Gordon finishes his story.

I could get used to this new policy, he thinks to himself. 'Very well, sir,' the Angel announces. 'Welcome to the kingdom of Heaven,' and he lets Gordon enter.

A few seconds later, Robin Cook comes up to the gate. The Angel is almost too shocked to speak. Thoughts of assassination and war pour through the Angel's head. Finally he says, 'Foreign Secretary, please tell me what it was like the day you died.'

Robin Cook says, 'OK, picture this. I'm naked inside a refrigerator…'

Robin Cook and John Prescott were talking about premarital sex and Prescott says to the Foreign Secretary: 'I never slept with my wife before marriage. Did you?'

Cook replies: 'I don't know, what was her maiden name?'

Cherie came into the room with a big smile and a spring in her step.

'My you're in a good mood,' said Tony. 'Why are you so happy?'

'I just got back from my annual physical exam and the doctor said I had the breasts of a 25-year-old woman, ' Cherie gushed.

'Did he say anything about your 46-year-old arse?' Tony asked.

'No,' said Cherie, 'your name wasn't mentioned once.'

Top Ten Excuses for Tony Blair's Disapproval Ratings

10 Middle-class people just don't understand his complex personality.

9 MI5 instigated rumours which are totally untrue and, besides, taken out of context.

8 Cherie Booth.

7 Today's apathetic youth just don't appreciate the finer points of socialist policy.

6   That Conservative-biased media.

5   Unexpectedly high deficits which can only be cured by unpopular Labour tax and spend policies.

4   Unpopularity is a sign of leadership.

3   Greedy Thatcher generation actually expects value for taxes.

2   Mandelson slipped his leash.

1   That receding hairline

Tony Blair was speaking at a business lunch in Tokyo, where he decided to open his speech with a brief joke. He told the joke, then waited for the translator to announce the Japanese version. Even though the story was quite short, Blair was surprised by how quickly the interpreter was able to re-tell it. Even more impressive was the reaction from the crowd. The Prime Minister thought the story was clever, but not outright hilarious, yet the crowd fell about laughing. Blair was very flattered. After the speech, he wanted to meet the translator. Perhaps there was a better way to tell the joke? When Blair asked how the joke had been told in Japanese, the translator responded, 'I told them, "Prime Minister Blair has told a very funny joke. Please laugh now."'

Mirror, Mirror, on the wall...

Top Ten Things Which Would Be Different if the Prime Minister Were a Dog

1 Labour Party HQ replaced by 20 storey high-fire hydrant
2 Abolition of Pets Mean Prizes
3 Capital punishment restored for Dale Winton
4 Doggy door on Number Ten
5 Dog biscuits on the NHS
6 Compulsory sterilization for all cats
7 Life sentences for tail dockers
8 Battersea Dog's Home to be renovated and to replace Chequers as PM's country residence
9 First Lady to be renamed First Bitch
10 PM to have the mandatory right to shag the legs of all fellow Cabinet Ministers

What's the Difference between Socialists and Conservatives?

Conservatives are Socialists with money.

Socialists believe property is theft. Conservatives believe everything is property.

Conservatives are bosses; Socialists work for them when they run out of other options.

Conservatives ride in stretch limos; Socialists throw bricks through their windscreens.

Conservatives go to the police after they've been mugged; Socialists get mugged by the police.

A Conservative wants to marry another Conservative, but only after sleeping with enough Socialists.

Socialists ignore the Inland Revenue; Conservatives hire accountants and attorneys to fight it.

Conservatives think the Government is trying steal the property they rightfully own; Socialists think the Government is trying to defend property that nobody rightfully owns.

Conservatives are organized in a political party; Socialists aren't organized in anything.

Conservatives think Socialists are naive and unrealistic; Socialists don't care what Conservatives think.

A bus load of politicians were driving down a country road, when all of a sudden, the bus ran off the road and crashed into a tree in an old farmer's field. The old farmer, after seeing what happened, went over to investigate. He then proceeded to dig a hole and bury the politicians.

A few days later, the local sheriff came out, saw the crashed bus, and asked the farmer where all the politicians had gone. The old farmer said he had buried them. The sheriff then asked the old farmer, 'Were they *all* dead?'

The old farmer replied, 'Well, some of them said they weren't, but you know how them politicians lie.'

The wives of four world leaders were having tea and the topic was raised of what one diplomatically calls a gentleman's 'manhood' in their language.

Tony Blair's wife said in England people call it a gentleman, because it stands up when women are entering.

Jaques Chirac's wife said in France you call it a curtain, because it goes down after the act.

Boris Yeltsin's wife said in Russia you call it a patriot, because you never know if it will hit you on the front or on the back side.

Hillary Clinton said that in the USA you call it a rumour, because it goes from mouth to mouth.

Saddam Hussein telephoned Tony Blair: 'Tony, I'm calling because last night I had the most beautiful dream. I could see the whole of London – it was wonderful and a flag waved above every house.'

The Prime Minister pondered for a moment and said: 'Saddam, what could you see on the flags?'

Saddam chuckled and replied: 'Allah is God, God is Allah.'

Blair immediately hit back: 'You know, Saddam, I'm really glad you called, because I had a similar dream last night too. I could see the whole of Baghdad, and it was even more beautiful than before the war, and every house had a flag.'

Saddam asked: 'Tony, what was on the flags?'

Blair replied: 'I don't know. I can't read Hebrew.'

Top Ten Signs Tony Blair Thinks He's Margaret Thatcher

1 Wanders round Number Ten shrieking 'Rejoice, Rejoice'
2 Keeps calling Alastair Campbell 'Bernard'
3 Keeps a close check on Euan's bank account
4 Keeps pouring gin and tonic down Cherie's neck
5 Describes Peter Mandelson as 'One of Them' as opposed to 'One of Us'
6 After Lords defeat on fox hunting announces 'I fight on. I fight to win'
7 Tells close confidant that 'Every Prime Minister Needs a Peter'
8 Gazes lovingly into US President's eyes at summit meeting
9 Upon meeting Boris Yeltsin declares: 'I like Mr Yeltsin. We can do business together'
10 Following Prescott's resignation a bewildered Blair describes him in interview with Brian Walden as 'unassailable'

John Prescott is on his way to New York. On the plane his advisers warn him about the cunning American journalists. Prescott reassures them: 'Don't worry – they won't get one over on me. But at JFK Airport a scrum of journalists are lying in wait.

One of them asks: 'Will you be visiting any lap-dancing clubs in New York, Mr Prescott?'

Prescott thinks for a minute and asks casually, 'Are there lap-dancing clubs here then?'

Headline in the *Daily News* the next day: 'Prescott's First Question: Are There Lap-Dancing Clubs Here Then?'

John Prescott decides to go to the opera with his wife. He gets to the ticket office and as he's not sure how ticketing works at an opera he asks the chap in front of him in the queue. He tells the Deputy PM he should do exactly what he does and everything would be OK.

He goes to the till and says: 'One ticket for *Tristan and Isolde* please.'

Prescott then reaches the till and says: 'And I'd like tickets for John and Pauline please.'

Frank Dobson and John Prescott go to the cinema to see a western starring John Wayne. During the film John Wayne rides past a hill in the desert. Prescott says: 'Dobbo, I bet you £100 that when he gets past the hill John Wayne will be surprised by an Indian and thrown from his horse.'

Dobson, liking a flutter, accepts the bet and bets £100 that he stays on the horse.

Indeed, behind the hill an Indian jumps out and the horse throws John Wayne to the ground.

When the film has finished and they are outside the cinema Dobson hands over the £100. Prescott looks rather sheepish and says: 'Frank, I've got to admit that I've seen the film before.'

Dobson smiles and proudly says: 'So have I!'

Prescott looks a bit shocked and asks: 'Well, why on earth did you take the bet on then?'

Dobson replied: 'I really couldn't believe that John Wayne would be so stupid as to let himself be surprised by the Indian behind the hill again.'

A tramp is considering how best he can get some money. Finally he comes to the conclusion that politicians are the only people who always seem to have money. So the next day he plonks himself down outside the Members' Entrance of the House of Commons and starts eating tufts of grass he has pulled out of St James's Park. Tony Blair walks by and asks: 'What on earth are you doing, why are you eating grass?'

The tramp looks up and says: 'Times are bad and that's all I have to eat.'

'Well, here's £10,' says the PM, 'go and buy yourself something decent to eat.'

The tramp gets up, walks along Whitehall, buys a six pack and drinks the lot with some mates under Waterloo Bridge. He relates what he did and one of his friends decides to try the same trick. Next morning he takes up his position outside the House of Commons and starts eating grass.

Norman Tebbitt walks past and asks what the tramp thinks he's doing. The tramp explains how times are bad and that he has nothing else to eat. Tebbitt considers this for a moment and then says: 'Well, here's £1.20 for the tube fair to Richmond Park. The grass is three feet high there...'

Tony Blair and John Prescott go for a walk up Oxford Street. Prescott says: 'Look at these prices! Trousers, £3, Suits £5. Our anti-inflation policies are really working!'

Blair looks to the heavens and says: 'You're looking in the window of a dry cleaners.'

A pheasant was standing in a field chatting to a bull. 'I would love to be able to get to the top of yonder tree,' sighed the pheasant, 'but I haven't got the energy.'

'Well, why don't you nibble on some of my droppings?' replied the bull. 'They're packed with nutrients.'

The pheasant pecked at them and found that they actually gave him enough strength to reach the first branch of the tree. The next day, after eating more, he reached the second branch. And so on. Finally, after a fortnight, there he was, proudly perched at the top of the tree.

Whereupon he was spotted by a farmer who dashed into the farmhouse, emerged with a shotgun, and shot the pheasant right out of the tree.

Moral of the story: Bulls*!t might get you to the top, but it won't keep you there!

Ron Davies and a big black guy go down to the riverside to take a leak. The black guy unzips his zipper and unloads this monster. Ron Davies can't resist a peak and says, 'Whoa! What's your name?'

The big guy says, 'Ben Brown.' Ron Davies faints dead away. The big guy gets done, bangs the head against a rock, loads it back in, and then grabs Ron and shakes him.

Ron looks up and says, 'What'd you say your name was?'

The big guy says, 'Ben Brown.'

Ron Davies says, 'Phew. I thought you said, "Bend down."'

Top Ten Least Popular Labour Party Conference Souvenirs

10 Gerald Kaufman kidney stone cuff links

9 Gift certificate for free backrub from Mo Mowlam

8 Bathmat made from Tony Banks's old hairpieces

7 Denis Healey's Unbelievably Low-impact Aerobics video

6 The 'I Support Gwynneth Dunwoody Wonderbra'

5 Honk if you have a sinking feeling this isn't our year bumpersticker

4 CD entitled *Sounds John Prescott Makes in the Morning*

3 Video of Andrew Smith's greatest speeches

2 I love Peter Mandelson badges

1 Frank Dobson's bacon-scented cologne

When the Liars' Club held their big meet,
Said Tony Blair, who was asked to compete,
'I can never take part,
Lacking skill in that art.'
All the others conceded defeat.

An Ode To New Labour

We are the New Labour Party
We strive to provide equity.
With effort unswerving
We help the deserving,
And they're none so deserving as we!

Through appropriate spin and cosmetic
Even Wales is seen as aesthetic.
So we called on Ron Davies
Whose lusts drove him crazy
Leaving Alun Michael looking quite pathetic.

To support many government hacks
The taxpayers were mercilously sacked.
These deeds grim and frown
Are told now by Brown
Who should know, since he led the attack.

For environment spare no expense,
And for sure give the poor recompense.
As we strive for the good
It is well understood
We have patronage jobs to dispense.

Clare Short is the crème de la crème.
This New Dame is no delicate femme.
Any chauvinist male
At her presence turns tail
For she shouts with the greatest of them.

High class criminals never need sweat
Where they'll pay back society's debt
If stark cells make them nervous
There's community service
Jack Straw'll see to that, you bet.

All business donations are cursed.
Tainted money helps them seek things perverse.
So that we just despise
Gifts from free enterprise,
Unless they are laundered well first.

Labour pups had been trained to bark,
'Long live Kinnock! Long live Kinnock! Long live Kinnock!'
But this din failed to last;
It's a thing of the past,
Since the pups now see more than the dark.

Job protection is sacred we trust
So no sacks that just may be unjust
This does widely apply
But not to a guy
Like Prescott, who's not one of us.

Gordon has told us, at least once or twice.
Acquiring much wealth is not nice
So his taxes don't hurt you
They just strengthen your virtue
As your leader protects you from vice.

Top Ten Reasons To Vote

1 The chance to take a deep breath in a high school gymnasium
2 Good practice for voting for a Song for Europe
3 So you'll feel personally involved when your MP is hauled off to gaol
4 Even though it's never come close to happening, your one vote could make a difference
5 You'll feel so self-righteous if the other lot get in and muck things up
6 If you don't vote you can't whinge about how terrible things are
7 You get a kick out of spoiling your ballot paper
8 You hate to be in the minority
9 You just love giving a false polling number to the saddos outside the polling station
10 If you can't beat em…

How many politicians does it take to change a light bulb?
Loads.

1 Tony Blair to point out that the light bulb has been smashed and destroyed by 18 years of Conservative Government

2 Jack Straw to explain to John Prescott that they know the light bulb needs changing because they're standing in the dark

3 Robin Cook to have a 'quick one' with someone else before the lights go back on

4 John Major to think up a solution to the problem, which is then rejected by everyone else

5 William Hague to explain to people that the Tories do care.

6 Edward Heath to explain to people that William Hague doesn't care

7 Michael Howard to point out that the pee-ple responsible for the evil destruction of the light bulb will suffer in prison.

8 Michael Portillo to get his knife ready to stab someone in the dark

9 Paddy Ashdown to mention that under the Liberal Democrats, the light bulb wouldn't have broken

10 Peter Mandelson will give advice on the screwing in

11 At the same time Ron Davies is trying to eat the light bulb

12 All whilst Ann Widdecombe has realised that the light bulb was fine, but the light-switch wasn't on

Robin Cook invites a young secretary into his office. She sees a 12-inch, shiny pen on his desk. 'Where did you get that?' she asks.

Cook says, 'I have a magic genie who gave it to me. Here, let me show you.' He pulls a genie out of his desk and asks the secretary to make a wish. She asks for a million bucks.

Suddenly thousands of ducks come quacking. 'What's going on – I said bucks, not ducks!'

Robin Cook replies, 'Oh, he's a little hard of hearing. I mean do you really think I asked him for a 12-inch BIC?'

More bad news for William Hague's quest to become president in 2000. Paula Jones claims he exposed himself to her in a hotel room and he has no distinguishing characteristics whatsoever.

Q: Why are the British more civilized than the Americans?
A: To greet their leader, they only go down on one knee.

'Rabinowich,' a friend asked, 'do you read New Labour newspapers?'

'Sure I do!' he responded. 'How else could I learn what a happy life I lead?'

Tony Blair gives a radio address to the British people: 'I have two important announcements for you – one joyful and one wistful. The wistful news is that during the next seven years we'll have nothing but bullshit. And the joyful one is that there will be an abundance of it.'

A doctor, an engineer, and a politician were arguing as to which profession was older. 'Well,' argued the doctor, 'without a physician mankind could not have survived, so I am sure that mine is the oldest profession.'

'No,' said the engineer, 'before life began there was complete chaos, and it took an engineer to create some semblance of order from this chaos. So engineering is older.'

'But,' chirped the triumphant politician, 'who created the chaos?'

Top Ten Signs Tony Blair Has Become 'Hip'

1 Loosens tie during intimate game with Cherie
2 Opens Prime Minister's Question Time with 'Awright Will?'
3 He's been shooting the shit with Liam Gallagher
4 Cherie's knackered, if you get the drift
5 Recently seen tapping foot to a Sister Sledge CD
6 Heard screaming abuse at the referee at a Newcastle soccer game
7 Tells Bill Clinton he inhaled
8 Swaps Ford Galaxy people mover for Audi Cabriolet
9 Annoys the neighbours with Def Leppard guitar impersonation
10 Repaints Number Ten door in turquoise

A politician to a woman, 'You look beautiful today!'

The woman replied, 'Thanks, but unfortunately I could not say the same about you.'

'Sure you could!' said the politician, 'if you could lie as well as I do!'

It is time to elect a world leader and your vote counts.
Here's the scoop on the three leading candidates:

Candidate A: associates with ward heelers and consults astrologists. He's had two mistresses. He chain-smokes and drinks eight to ten martinis a day.

Candidate B: was kicked out of office twice, sleeps until noon, used opium in college and drinks a quart of brandy every evening.

Candidate C: is a decorated war hero. He's a vegetarian, doesn't smoke, drinks an occasional beer and hasn't had any illicit affairs.

Which of these candidates is your choice?
Candidate A is Franklin D. Roosevelt
Candidate B is Winston Churchill
Candidate C is Adolph Hitler

One Friday morning, a teacher came up with a novel way to motivate her class. She told them that she would read a quote and the first student to correctly identify who said it would receive the rest of the day off.

She started with 'This was England's finest hour.' Little Suzy instantly jumped up and said, 'Winston Churchill.'

'Congratulations,' said the teacher, 'you may go home early.'

The teacher then said, 'Ask not what your country can do for you, but…' Before she could finish the quote, another young lady belts out, 'John F. Kennedy!'

'Very good,' says the teacher, 'you may go also.'

Irritated that he has missed two golden opportunities, Little Johnny said, 'I wish those girls would just shut up.'

Upon overhearing this comment, the outraged teacher demanded to know who said it. Instantly Johnny rose to his feet and said, 'Joe Ashton and Robin Cook. I'll see you Monday.'

This little old lady calls 999. When the operator answers she yells: 'Help, send the police to my house right away! There's a damn Socialist on my front porch and he's playing with himself.'

'What?' the operator exclaimed.

'I said there is a damn Socialist on my front porch playing with himself and he's weird; I don't know him and I'm afraid! Please send the police!' the little old lady repeated.

'Well, now, how do you know he's a Socialist?'

'Because, you damn fool, if it was a Conservative, he'd be screwing somebody!'

The Lord said to Noah, 'In six months, I'm going to make it rain until the earth is covered with water and all the evil is destroyed. I want you to build an ark and save two of each animal species. Here are the blueprints for the ark.'

Six months passed. The skies began to cloud and rain began to fall. Noah sat in his front garden, weeping.

'Why haven't you built the ark?' asked the Lord.

'Oh, forgive me,' said Noah. 'I did my best, but so many things happened. The blueprints you gave me didn't meet the council's code and I had to change them. Then the council said I was violating the zoning ordinance by building an ark in my front garden, so I had to get an exemption. The Forestry Commission required tree-cutting permits, and I was sued by an animal rights group when I tried to gather up the animals. The Environment Agency required an environmental impact statement concerning the flood. The Army Corps of Engineers wanted a map of the proposed flood plain. The Inland Revenue seized all my assets, claiming I was trying to avoid paying taxes by leaving the country, and the Equal Opportunity Commission said I wasn't hiring enough ethnic minorities. I'm sorry, Lord, but I can't finish the ark for at least five years.'

Suddenly the rain stopped, the skies cleared and the sun began to shine. Noah looked up and said, 'Lord, does this mean you're not going to devastate the earth?'

'Right,' said the Lord. 'The government already has.'

Some time ago President Clinton was hosting a state dinner for Prime Minister Tony Blair when, at the last minute, his regular cook took ill and they had to get a replacement at short notice. The fellow arrived and turned out to be a very grubby looking man named Jon. The President voiced his concerns to his chief of staff but was told that this was the best they could do at such short notice. Just before the meal, the President noticed the cook sticking his fingers in the soup to taste it and again he complained to the chief of staff about the cook, but he was told that this man was supposed to be a very good chef.

The meal went OK but the President was sure that the soup tasted a little off, and by the time dessert came, he was starting to have stomach cramps and nausea. It was getting worse and worse till finally he had to excuse himself from the state dinner to look for the bathroom. Passing through the kitchen, he caught sight of the cook, Jon, scratching his rear end and this made him feel even worse. By now he was desperately ill with violent cramps and was so disorientated that he couldn't remember which door led to the bathroom.

He was on the verge of passing out from the pain when he finally found a door that opened and as he undid his trousers and ran in, he realized to his horror that he had stumbled into Monica Lewinsky's office with his trousers around his knees. As he was just about to pass out, she bent over him and heard her President whisper in a barely audible voice, 'Sack my cook.' And that is how the whole misunderstanding occurred.

Q: What is green, has four legs and smells like woman?
A: Robin Cook's pool table.

One night, on a visit to Washington, Tony Blair was invited to stay overnight in the Lincoln Bedroom at the White House. Suddenly, at 4 am he was awakened by George Washington's ghost. 'George, what is the best thing I could do to help my country?' Blair asked.

'Set an honest and honourable example, just as I did,' advised George.

The next night the ghost of Thomas Jefferson moved through the dark bedroom. 'Tom, what is the best thing I could do to help the country?' Blair asked.

'Cut taxes and reduce the size of government,' advised Tom.

Blair didn't sleep well the next night, and saw yet another figure moving in the shadows. It was Abraham Lincoln's ghost. 'Abe, what is the best thing I could do to help the country?' Blair asked.

Abe replied, 'Go to the theatre.'

A woman shows up at Ron Davies's house in a trench coat and scarf and says: 'I received your emergency phone call, Mrs Davies, and came right away, but what could I possibly do to save your husband's career?'

Mrs Davies said: 'Come inside and let me explain, Mrs Bobbit…'

Q: Why are politicians like nappies?
A: Both should be changed regularly and for the same reason.

A little girl asked her father, 'Daddy? Do all fairy tales begin with Once Upon a Time?'

And he replied, 'No, there is a whole series of fairy tales that begin with 'If elected I promise…''

Top Ten Ways to Make William Hague more Exciting

1   Kill a man with kung fu kick on *Panorama*
2   Dump Ffion and marry her 14-year-old cousin
3   Change campaign slogan from 'Fresh Start' to 'Fresh Beaver'
4   Answer questions on *Question Time* with 'D'know, I was too pissed to remember'
5   Hang out with Liam Gallagher
6   Shave head completely – might as well anyway
7   Outdo Blair by refusing to use nouns as well as verbs
8   Take weekend break on Club 18–30 holiday in Benidorm
9   Go to celeb party with Tiffany from *Eastenders* and describe as a 'Perfect Moment'
10 Go on *Stars in Their Eyes* and say, 'And tonight Matthew, I'm going to be Shirley Bassey'

The Labour Party announced today that they are changing their emblem from a rose to a condom because it more clearly reflects their party's political stance. A condom stands up to inflation, halts production, discourages co-operation, protects a bunch of dicks, and gives one a sense of security while screwing others.

One night, after a long hard day at work a politician went home. It was fairly late, around 10 p.m. All of the sudden, a masked man jumped out of the bushes and demanded all the politician's money.

'You can't do that!' The politician cried. 'I'm a politician!'

'Oh,' said the masked man, 'in that case give me all *my* money!!'

A Martian landed in the country. He went up to a farmhouse and knocked on the door. He told the farmer he would give him a million pounds for his flock of sheep. The farmer said OK. The Martian pulled a tiny sheep out of his pocket and it ate all the sheep. The Martian then offered the farmer two million pounds for all his cattle. He pulled a tiny cow from his pocket and it ate all the cattle.

The farmer said: 'I will give you all the money back if you can pull a tiny Conservative from your pocket.'

Q: What's the difference between crime and politics?
A: In politics, you take the money and run, but for re-election.

Ten Signs Cherie Booth Thinks She's Hillary Clinton

1 She expresses a desire to reform the National Health Service personally
2 She denies murdering the Attorney General
3 Always got a downer on Chelsea
4 Looks at her husband in that doe-eyed kind of a way
5 Holds hands with her husband in public
6 Goes pale at Tony's suggestion for a whitewater rafting holiday
7 Wears a badge saying 'Proud to be a Lawyer'
8 Urges Tony to get a tattoo down below just like Bill's
9 Puts phone down upon hearing the words: 'Hi, I'm Paula Jones'
10 Doesn't like these secret meetings with a blonde called Margaret

Most politicians have three hats: one to wear, one to toss in the ring, and the third, to talk through.

A recent visitor to Whitehall scanned the street up and down, then finally asked a local, 'Can you tell me which side the Foreign Office is on?'

'Ours, I think...' replied a passer-by, 'but lately, I'm not all that sure.'

The local bar was so sure that its bartender was the strongest man around that it offered a standing £1,000 bet.

The bartender would squeeze a lemon until all the juice ran into a glass, and hand the lemon to a patron. Anyone who could squeeze one more drop of juice out would win the money. Many people had tried over time (weight-lifters, dockers, etc.) but nobody could do it.

One day a stooping, dark-haired man came into the bar, and said: 'I'd like to try the bet.'

After the laughter had died down, the bartender said OK, grabbed a lemon, and squeezed away. Then he handed the wrinkled remains of the rind to the little man.

But the crowd's laughter turned to total silence as the man clenched his fist around the lemon and six drops fell into the glass.

As the crowd cheered, the bartender paid the £1,000, and asked the little man, 'What do you do for a living? Are you a lumberjack, a weight-lifter, or what?'

The man replied, 'I'm the Chancellor of the Exchequer.'

Top Ten Good Things About Being Prime Minister

1 Every day, your weight in 10ps from the Dartford Tunnel toll booth
2 It's the second most powerful position in the country – behind the editor of the *Sun*
3 Full control of the nuclear arsenal, aimed at a country of your prejudice
4 You're not married to Pauline Prescott
5 Being able to visit high school gymnasiums at a time of your choice
6 People always telling you what you want to hear
7 Being able to spend, spend, spend
8 You finally get to settle all those scores
9 Subscription-free access to CNN
10 Speeding through red lights in a chauffeur-driven Daimler

Conservatives and Socialists: how to tell them apart

Conservative women usually wear hats. Socialists usually don't.

Socialists buy banned books. Conservatives form censorship committees and read them.

Socialists eat the fish they catch. Conservatives hang them on the wall.

Conservatives study the financial pages of the newspaper. Socialists put them on the bottom of the bird cage.

On Saturday, Conservatives head for the golf course, the yacht club, or the hunting lodge. Socialists get a haircut, wash the car, or go bowling.

Conservatives have guest rooms. Socialists have spare rooms filled with old baby furniture.

Conservatives hire exterminators. Socialists step on the bugs.

Conservatives sleep in twin beds – some even in separate rooms. That is why there are more Socialists.

Top Ten Ways Cherie Blair Could Improve Her Image

1 Move her eyes closer together
2 Never be seen with Hillary Clinton
3 Appear on TV as Julia Brogan in *Brookside*
4 Have an operation to remove the 666 from her scalp
5 Make prank call to Tony on the *Jimmy Young Show* pretending to be a secret lover
6 Stop wearing the 'All prime ministers are stupid' T Shirt
7 Comb her hair
8 Get rid of *that* nightie
9 When kissing Tony in public, get the timing right
10 Learn to buy her kids some decent clothes

Political Anagrams

Anthony Blair	Tory Hannibal
Anthony Charles Lynton Blair	Hi! Harlot nanny robs rectally Tally-ho! Nato ran in. Lynch Serb! Born actor. Lethally nanny-ish Tall choir-boy nanny enthrals Tory nob. Heal-all nanny. Christ Nonchalantly slithery baton Lynch nationals abhorrently A tall, nanny-ish, crony brothel Nob nanny-ish harlot rectally Tyrannic rant all boloney: shh! Nonchalantly is abhorrently Nonchalently nasty, horrible.
Anthony Neil Wedgwood Benn	Own an enlightened body now!
Bernie Eccleston	Recent obscene lie Obscene lie centre
Betty Boothroyd	Tory hot body Bet!
Betty Boothroyd Speaker	Keep bad Tory Boys Hotter
Cool Britannia	Blair! No action

128

Dennis Skinner	Inner kindness Skinned sinner
Humphrey the Downing Street Cat	Cherie wants mog hurt. The end pet!
James Gordon Brown	Now more grand jobs
John Leslie Prescott	Nice hot polls jester

Ken Livingstone	Votes Lenin King
Kenneth Robert Livingstone	Inherent voter bonking. Let's! Not in the knob list revenger Enlighten voter – insert knob
Labour Party Conference	Unenforceable Tory crap
Liberal Democrats	Creditable morals Miserable cold rat Dismal rectal bore
Margaret Thatcher	A girl: the arch mad hatter Ha! The arch rich mad tart
Michael Heseltine	Elect him. He's an alien!
Michael Portillo	A cool limp Hitler
New Labour	War on Blue
New Labour is Working	Brown is our weakling OK burglaries win now
Paddy Ashdown	Ah! Odd SDP yawn!

Peter Mandelson	Resent dome plan
	Lamented person
	Lean modern pest
	Tamed personnel
	Plans? Enter dome
	Personal dement
Prime Minister Tony Blair	Slimier rent-boy in armpit
	I'm irritably omnipresent
	Blimey! I'm irritant person
Robin Cook Foreign Secretary	FO Boy – erection error, sacking!
Robin Finlayson-Cook	Sick on no-brain loony
Ron Davies MP	I'm no sad perv
Roy Hattersley	The Tory slayer
	There's royalty?
Rt Hon William Hague MP	The human wimp gorilla
	Oh! I'm a well-hung armpit
	I'm the low glum piranha
Scottish National Party	Oh! Nasty tartan politics

Shirley Williams	I whirl aimlessly
The Conservative Party	Teacher in vast poverty Reach vain petty voters Reactivate NHS poverty Tap in the vast recovery Votes threaten privacy
The Conservative Party Conference	French contraceptive on every seat?
The Labour Manifesto	O this beaten formula Tories unfathomable Am I not boastful here?
The Labour Party	Prole? Bury that Upbeat harlotry Blather up a Tory A bluer Tory path
The Labour Party Conference	No perfect Tory unreachable Act clean! Probe Fuehrer Tony!
The Millennium Dome	I'm dull. I'm one theme

The National Health Service	Hosanna! Evil Thatcher elite The vain anaesthetic or hell Enhance this volatile heart
The New Labour Party	Power hunt! Betrayal
The Right Honourable William Hague	Oh hurrah, I'm a well-hung elite bigot
Tony Blair	Tory in Lab Not by Rail Only a Brit A Lib 'n' Tory All mediocre brats
Tony Blair Labour Leader	Badly unreliable orator
Tony Blair PM	I'm Tory Plan B
Virginia Bottomley	I'm an evil Tory bigot
William Hague	I'm a huge walli
William Hague MP	I'm all huge wimp